The
ETERNAL
BUDDHA

IRH Press

BOOKS
IRH PRESS
New York

ISBN: 978-1-958655-19-1

Printed in Canada

First Edition

The
ETERNAL
BUDDHA

Now, Here,
Is the Imperishable Light

EL CANTARE

RYUHO OKAWA

IRH Press

Contents

Preface (revised edition) 11

Preface (original edition) 12

CHAPTER ONE

Awaken

The Proof That You Are Buddha's Disciples 14

The Importance of Believing 17

Know the Parent of Your Soul 21

Because Buddha's Teachings Exist 24

Open the Window of Your Mind 29

The Lifeline Called Faith 33

Fulfill Your Vows to Buddha 38

CHAPTER TWO

Become a Person of Truth

Live Honestly 44

The Right Value Standards 51

In Proportion to Your Efforts 55

Live Your Own Life to the Fullest 60

Reap the Best Fruit Possible 63

The Joy in Receiving No Reward 69

The Joy of Buddha 73

The True Desire of Buddha's Disciples 77

CHAPTER THREE

Imperishable Power

Diligent Efforts 82

The Greatest Delight in Life 87

The Work of the Sangha 91

The True Meaning of Missionary Work 94

The Primary Vow of Buddha 101

Prescription for the Soul 107

The Path of Giving Back 111

Bodhisattvas of the Earth 114

CHAPTER FOUR

The Time to Make a Leap

A Time of Miracles 118

True Equality and Freedom 125

The Root of the Soul 131

Search Out the Gold Coin 136

The Path of Right Thought 140

Washing the Fabric of Your Soul 145

When the Soul Makes a Great Leap 150

CHAPTER FIVE

The Eternal Buddha

I Am Greater Than a Savior 154

Buddha Is the Laws and Also the Teachings 157

One Hundred Billion Years of History 162

The Moment of Glory 165

The Choice of Humankind 168

Be Brave and Stand Up 172

Now, Here, Is the Light of the Eternal Buddha 176

Afterword (original edition)............................. 179

Afterword (revised edition)............................. 180

About the Author 183

Books by Ryuho Okawa 184

Music by Ryuho Okawa 191

Who Is El Cantare? 192

About Happy Science 194

Happy Science's English Sutra 196

Memberships 197

Contact Information 198

About IRH Press USA Inc. 200

Preface (revised edition)

Buddha's teachings are the expression of the deep and profound Truth that is conveyed in simple words.

For this reason, they are *the supreme.*

They teach the laws of the mind in a way that suits people of all levels as if to cast a wide net.

For this reason, they are *the greatest.*

Moreover, they are preached with words that are filled with unwavering, quiet confidence.

For this reason, they are *the most powerful.*

The Laws of the Eternal Buddha merge boundless sacred mysteries with crystal-clear logic and flow endlessly like the waters of the Ganges River.

The Truth that was taught 2,500 years ago is still the Truth today and will remain the Truth 3,000 years from now.

For this reason, it is called *the most victorious.*

> *Ryuho Okawa*
> *Master & CEO of Happy Science Group*
> *Midsummer 1999*

Preface (original edition)

Following *The Rebirth of Buddha*, I present this book, *The Eternal Buddha*, to the world.

This book contains the supreme, the greatest, and the most powerful teachings of all, and is, therefore, the most victorious.

With this book in your hands, and when you read through the pages, you will surely gain victory. Those who read, savor, understand, and practice the teachings in this book will never be defeated in life. The greatest moment is in your hands here, right now.

Take your time and really savor this book. When you do, you will realize that you are not just a simple mass of physical matter, but rather, an eternal being shining with golden light.

> *Ryuho Okawa*
> *Master & CEO of Happy Science Group*
> *July 1991*

CHAPTER ONE

Awaken

The Proof That You Are Buddha's Disciples

All of you, my disciples,
I shall once again give you
An important message.

Many of you have now lived a few decades on earth,
And must have probably forgotten
The soul training you have continued doing
In your past lives.
But I will say unto you,
Throughout your numerous past reincarnations,
You lived your life as disciples of Buddha.
In the long, long period of many reincarnations,
You lived as my disciples.

Look deep within your hearts.
Then, you will find that you are longing for something
Deeply and strongly.
It is a strong yearning for a path.
You have a desire
To live strongly for something noble
No matter how tough the path may be.
This strong desire
Is your aspiration for enlightenment.

This aspiration for enlightenment in your hearts
Is proof that you were once my disciples.
Look within yourselves,
And should you find
A strong aspiration for enlightenment
Or even a faint but significant feeling of longing
That lies at the depth of your heart,
You can be assured

That you were my disciple in the past.

Yes, you are the ones

That I wish to share these important words.

The Importance of Believing

What I would like to speak to you first
Is about the importance of believing.

Sometimes, you may be confused
And your hearts may be shaken
By all kinds of values around you.
However, the act of believing, in itself,
Speaks confidently of the fact
That you are all beings beyond this world.
Deep within, everyone has the heart to believe
And the desire to believe.
By this, I do not mean
The desire to believe in something of this world.
It is the desire to believe
In a world far beyond this one
And the wisdom that is stored there.

Many people of the modern age
Seem to arrogantly believe that
Everything can be understood
Through their own intellect;
They have become arrogant and full of pride.
However, should these modern people
Look deep within their hearts,
They will know that they are
Ardently looking for something
That is beyond their comprehension.
They will not be able to close those eyes
That are desperately looking for the Truth
No matter how hard they try.

No matter how knowledgeable
People may say you are in this world,
Just look up at the night sky.

Can you explain the wonders of the stars
Scattered across the sky?
Can you explain why the Earth is round,
Or why it rotates on its own?
Can you explain why the sun always rises in the east
And sets in the west?
What lies at the depth of all this
Is Buddha's great love for all people
Who will go through soul training in this world.
Even if those who are undergoing soul training
Do not notice,
This great form of love continues to manifest itself,
Granting people an environment to live in.
You must realize and feel this magnificent love.

The wonders of Mother Nature.
The mystery of the Great Universe.
Even if humans do not understand them,

They continue to nurture humankind.

Ah, if you find yourself being moved by them,

Even by a little,

Believing should surprisingly be a simple task for you.

Belief is, first, the overflowing feeling

That wells up from the depths of your soul

When you discover that

You are being allowed to live.

When you realize this fact,

Your longing for the Truth

Will seek further

For what lies beyond these wonders.

Know the Parent of Your Soul

Yes, this is only natural.

Doesn't a newborn baby

Seek to know his mother and father?

There is nothing more saddening

For a child to be born into this world and grow up

Without knowing his mother and father.

A small, small baby cries for his mother

Without being taught to do so.

When a child cries out for his mother and father,

He learns who his guardians are.

No one teaches the child to do this.

The very fact of being alive,

The very act of living itself,

The very act of discovering that

You are being allowed to live

Will make you want to know who your parents are.

A log being washed downstream
Might not think at all,
But it is only natural for humans
With life and blood flowing through them
To wish to know who gave them life.

And when humans learn
That Buddha is the parent of their souls,
They, who are His children,
Can no longer live their lives
Without calling the parent's name.
Thus, people who have awakened to this truth
Will never stop calling for Buddha
Day after day.
Like a young child crying out
For their mother and father every day,
They will tirelessly call for Buddha.

You, too, are a small humble life
Born on this small planet called Earth.
If so,
Seek, seek.
Seek all things from your parent,
From the parent of your soul.
And all things shall be given to you.
No, they have already been given to you.
To realize this,
You must know the parent of your soul.
You must call out for Buddha.

Because Buddha's Teachings Exist

And then ponder this:

Why have you, human beings,

Been given the ability to think?

Why are you capable of thinking?

Why are you capable of making decisions?

Why are you capable of taking action?

It is because you fundamentally have

An ideal within that you believe in.

It is because you believe

That certain thoughts and certain actions

Are required of you

As the work of human beings.

Then, why do you think that way?

How did you come to that conclusion?

Why is it that you are able to think in the first place?

Is it not because the parent of your soul has

Descended to earth
And has been giving you the Teachings
As the Great Buddha?
Is it not true
That humankind learned what is right and wrong,
Only because Buddha has preached the Teachings?
Is it not true
That all fields of study
Began only after the Laws were preached?

In the Great Universe,
This Earth is no more than a grain of sand.
How, then, did the souls born on Earth
Acquire high-level values?
Was it purely by coincidence?
It must be because,
For thousands, tens of thousands,
Hundreds of thousands,

And millions of years, or even longer,

The Buddha incarnate

Continued to preach His Teachings

And left them as the Laws for humankind.

This was the beginning

Of the establishment of human souls.

It is thanks to the Laws

That you are able to live happily,

Day by day, without worry.

If you did not know the standards

By which to live your lives,

You would be at a loss every day.

However, because the Laws show you the right path,

You are able to walk through your life in peace,

Even if it is surrounded by darkness.

In this way,

The Teachings of Buddha become the Laws

And bring light to the travelers—

Yes, that is all of you—
Who are journeying through the dark night.
The Laws cast light onto all of you,
Who live in a world without light.

Faith is
To know this light.
Faith is
To know that this light is the light of the Laws.
Faith is
To know that this light of the Laws is the light of Love.
Faith is
To know that this light of the Laws is
Light full of Mercy.
Faith is
To know that this light comes from Buddha.
Faith is
To believe that this light shines onto this earth

Through Buddha,

Who is the Primordial Buddha of the Great Universe.

These are the source of all things.

Without acknowledging these facts,

You cannot claim that you have lived out your life

As a human being.

To be able to say that you have lived out your life

As a human being,

The record of your soul must show

That you have lived your life exploring Right Mind.

The Exploration of Right Mind

Is a duty as a human being,

And to fulfill this duty,

You must devote yourself to Buddha's Teachings.

Only by devoting yourself to the Teachings

Will all facts be revealed to you.

Open the Window of Your Mind

When the Master teaches the Laws,

He teaches in accordance with

The level of his disciples' minds.

Disciples must humbly open their minds

To learn the many of their Master's Teachings.

If they do not humbly open the window of their minds,

The light of Truth will not reach them.

If it does not reach your mind,

That is not the light's fault.

It is your own fault;

Your delusion of the mind has shut out the light.

You must get rid of this delusion.

Unless you get rid of all the delusions

That you formed from

The ideas and beliefs you acquired,

The education you received,

And the family circumstances
You were raised in
Since childhood,
The voice of Buddha will never reach your minds.
Open your minds
And learn the Teachings with an accepting heart.
Only then will you discover the direction
Your souls seek.

The joy that your soul experiences from this
Is unexchangeable.
The joy of discovering the Truth
Is more precious than any treasure.
Should a mountain of gold and treasure
Be piled before you,
Do not be captivated by it.
Should you be offered a great position in life,
Do not let your heart be wavered by it.

Should society laugh at you and mock you,
Do not let your heart be shaken.

I have taught you time and time again.
The most important thing for all of you
Is to raise the level of your souls.
You must choose things
That will nourish your souls.
The joy of the soul
Must be the greatest joy of your lives.
Therefore, do not be distracted
By things that do not serve as
Nourishment or nutrition for your souls.

It is good to distance yourselves
From fame and prestige.
Distance yourselves from earthly praise.
Know that

Should you be captivated by these things

And be unwilling to listen to the true Teachings,

You can only live like the stalks of reeds

That grow on the riverbank,

Trembling in the wind of impermanence.

If you are a human being with life,

Or a noble human being,

You must prioritize the joy of knowing the Laws

Above all happiness.

The Lifeline Called Faith

Also, you must never forget
Your faith and devotion to Buddha,
Who teaches the Laws.

To pledge devotion is
To know the attitude a disciple should have
To receive the Teachings.
It is to establish in yourselves
The attitude of a disciple.
It is to show respect to your Master
And walk the path of a disciple.
This is what it means to pledge devotion.

Faith is to honor the grand river of Truth
That flows from the Master.
It is to accept the Laws reverently

And make a vow to the Ultimate Buddha.
As you encountered the Truth
And were born anew as disciples of Buddha,
Vow to surely live a life of giving back.
Vow to surely live your lives
With the Teachings as your guide.
By making these vows and pledges,
Your faith becomes real.

Even if a rock that weighs tons
Tumbles down from above
And crushes your body,
Never give up on climbing the cliff
For the sake of the Truth.
Do not let go of the only lifeline
That hangs from the cliff.
That lifeline is called faith.
Even if your body is smashed into pieces

By a large rock,

Even if you are eaten by a thousand lions,

Even if your eyes are gouged by ten thousand eagles,

Never let go of the lifeline called faith.

You may lose your physical body,

Fame, social status, and wealth,

But as long as you are connected to Buddha

By the lifeline of faith,

You will never lose your eternal life.

However, the moment you let go of this lifeline,

You shall find yourself falling,

But not to the ground of this earth.

Alas, what awaits you is an infinite abyss of darkness.

Forever and ever shall you fall

Into the dark abyss called hell.

You would rather have your organs

Devoured by a lion

Than to lose faith

And fall into the very depths of hell.

You would rather endure the pain of an eagle

Gouging out your eyes

Than to suffer such a fate.

Hell is the death of the soul.

Only by letting your souls live

Can you thank and repay Buddha.

You have been granted lives as precious as diamonds.

Yet, do you intend to throw your lives into the sewer?

No, you must never.

You must all be strong.

You must all grow stronger through believing.

Faith will make you strong.

Not once has faith made you weak in the past.

Those who truly believe will be strong.

If you remain weak,

No matter how much you believe,
You are yet to have real faith.

You all must know that the lifeline,
The rope that you are holding onto,
Is a part of my robe.
As long as you hold on to that lifeline,
Buddha and His disciples shall be one.
Just as Buddha has never been defeated
In this world,
Neither will any of you be defeated.
Just as Buddha has never failed
To fulfill His oath in this world,
Neither will any of you
Fail to fulfill your oaths.

Fulfill Your Vows to Buddha

All of you must know
The Will of Buddha
And the Desire of Buddha.
That is to bring salvation
To all humankind on earth.
It is to save all people
Without leaving a single person behind.
The Desire of Buddha is to save,
Not only the people living in this lifetime,
But also those living in the other world
And even those who will be born into this world later.

Therefore, my disciples,
Your mission should be clear to you.
There is no other choice for you
But to walk this path together.

That is why I teach you the Laws as nourishment.

My Teachings are the nourishment for your souls.

As long as you feed on my Teachings,

You will not collapse on the path due to hunger.

As long as you live with these Teachings

As fertilizer and nourishment for your souls,

Limitless power and boundless passion

Shall well up from within you.

Make a vow to study

All the Teachings that flow out from Buddha.

Strive to thoroughly learn

Every single piece of Truth

That flows out from Buddha.

Only then can you gain infinite power.

If you wish to walk the long, distant path,

Acquire this power.

Feed on everything that nourishes your soul

Without leaving a single piece behind.
And walk the eternal path together.

All of you came down to this world
To save all people.
You were born on this land
And into this age
To rid all unhappiness from this world.
So, fulfill the vows you made to Buddha.
Vows made between Buddha and His disciples
Will always be fulfilled.

Awaken, awaken.
Be strong, be strong.
Believe, believe.
The path shall open up before you.
Walk this path steadily and tirelessly.
I am with you all.

I am walking the path carrying all of you on my back.
Never forget this.

CHAPTER TWO

Become a Person of Truth

Live Honestly

All of you, my disciples,

I have a message for you.

Always keep these words with you

And engrave them in your heart.

You must become a person of truth.

You must become a person who lives by the truth.

You must know that there is no other way

But to walk straightly, on and on

With the truth as your guide.

First, you must not lie.

Commit to living honestly.

Even in times when living honestly

Appears foolish from a worldly perspective,

You must still stick to living honestly.

Some people lie to get through life,

And it may seem that they are reaping credit,

Time and time again.

However, I say unto you,

People who use lies to get by in life

Will never succeed in the truest sense.

Others will eventually see through their lies

And these liars will be humiliated.

And in most cases,

This will happen during their life on earth.

But if by any chance,

They get away with lying in this lifetime,

There is the afterlife.

What is most scary about the afterlife

Is that not a single lie will be let off the hook there.

Unless you have the mind of a bodhisattva,

You cannot live in the world of bodhisattvas.

Likewise, ogres live in hell

Because they have the minds of an ogre.
Therefore, be forewarned.
No lie, deceit, or excuse
Will work in your favor
In the world beyond this one.

And on earth, too,
Your true nature will appear precisely
In your thoughts and actions.
You may insist that you cannot be recognized
In this world
Unless you use lies and deceit,
But any success achieved through them
Will eventually be unmasked
And cast into the abyss.
Thus, people who live honestly
Will ultimately win.
Never forget this truth.

However, you might ask me,
"How can we live honestly?
What does that exactly mean?"
You may wonder,
"What defines an honest life?
What defines a deceitful life?"

Indeed, many people are living
Without knowing that
They are living deceitfully.
They do not realize that
Their lives are fake.
However, observe them well.
People who unknowingly live a deceitful life
Share a common trait.
That is, they see everything only through
Worldly standards.

They love social status, fame, and wealth
Above all things,
And they do not acknowledge
How important their own minds are.
That is their trait.

If the success that people have earned
Is through much effort they made
And they continue to live for others' sake,
I would not say that their social status, fame,
Or wealth are wrong at all.
When these things are judged reasonable
By people around them,
It means these things have that much light.
It means people feel that much true joy in them.
However, you must be aware of foolish people
Who only evaluate their own worth
Based on things that can easily be seen by other people.

Some people are under the illusion
That they are great people
Because they live in big houses
Or because they drive around in expensive cars.
There are such people,
Which is why I say you should be careful.
Do not put the cart before the horse.
Only when people's minds and ways of life
Are truly valuable as human beings
Will the worldly means they have truly shine.
Do not misunderstand this order.

At the very least,
People who have never thought about
Their own state of mind
Will not even understand
What it means to live honestly, to begin with,
Because to live honestly means

To live in tune with your own conscience.

And to live in tune with your conscience is

To live in tune with

The voice of your guardian spirit deep within.

Your guardian spirits will then

Have to guide you

According to the will of higher spirits

Who are above them.

This is the essential meaning of living honestly.

And above it all is Buddha.

To live honestly is

To live with Buddha's Will as your own.

However, it is difficult

For most people to understand this,

So, it is commonly explained

As living in tune with your conscience.

The Right Value Standards

Think about it.

When you look back on the thoughts you had,

You may sometimes feel ashamed of some thoughts,

And sometimes feel proud of other thoughts.

Why is it that you feel ashamed of some

But proud of others?

This judgment rests on the conscience

That is within you all.

And the fact of having this conscience

Is undeniable proof that you are children of Buddha.

Because you are children of Buddha,

You all have the value standards of goodness itself

Inherent in you.

Thus, you must always be aware

Of the standard of righteousness

That you have in your mind.
You may be able to deceive others,
But you cannot deceive yourselves.
You know every thought you harbored
And every action you took,
So you must examine
Your thoughts and actions as they are
And not live your life in a shameful way.

Even if you may appear to be speaking good words
And doing good deeds from the outside,
If you have bad thoughts in your mind
And your true desire is
To corrupt or ruin people
By deceiving them,
Then, at the very least,
Your acts are not the acts of a heavenly being,
Regardless of whether others

Appreciate them or not.

You must acquire this right habit
As quickly as possible.
In the afterlife that is to come,
Even the slightest lies will not be accepted.
So get rid of all deceit while you are still alive
And live honestly.

In my eyes,
I see many people struggling in their lives.
I want to ask them,
"Why do you try to be more than who you are?"
"Why do you try to live a pretentious life?"
"Are you truly happy pretending to be
Someone you are not?"
This is not how you should be.
Only when people become proud of themselves for

Who they really are
Can they attain true happiness.
All human beings have a sense of inferiority.
However, you must not live a life of pretense
To hide your sense of inferiority
And go out of your way
To make yourself seem great.
A life of pretense
Will eventually make you stumble.

Each and every person
Has a way of life that feels natural to them.
There is a way of life they can be themselves.
Only by living in such a way
Can they live happily and carefree every day.
Each person has their own Middle Way.
Discovering your Middle Way
Is what is important.

In Proportion to Your Efforts

One thing that leads people astray
From the Middle Way
Is jealousy toward others.
The feeling of jealousy, an envious mind,
Will never make you happy.
You must know this.
Jealousy is a snake with venomous fangs.
Once it sneaks into your mind,
You will have sleepless nights.
Your mind will never be at ease,
As you will always be envious of others.

Remember this well.
You must not invite this venomous snake
Into your mind.
Jealousy must be nipped in the bud.

To nip jealousy in the bud,
You must evaluate people fairly.

Long, long ago,
You, as well as all other people,
Were granted human lives
As children of Buddha.
Since then, and until this day, you have been reborn
Thousands or tens of thousands of times,
Or perhaps even more than that.
You have accumulated that many lives.
Some of you have always lived
For the happiness of other people.
Some of you have always lived while
Hurting many people.
If both types of people were treated equally,
The world Buddha created
Would only be unfair and unjust.

Through all the reincarnations
Each person's soul has gone through,
They have each developed their own capacity.
To deny the capacity of other people's souls
That they developed in their past countless lives,
Is the same as denying other people's efforts.
Such people are ruled by a dark, tyrant-like mind.

Surely, you all have heard
The story of the ant and the grasshopper.
The ant worked hard and tirelessly all summer long
To gather and store food,
But the grasshopper did not.
Then, the ant asked the grasshopper,
"Mr. Grasshopper,
Shouldn't you be preparing for the future
Instead of singing all day long?"
But the grasshopper simply spent his life

Enjoying each day thinking,
"Tomorrow is another day."
Eventually, the leaves fell,
Autumn winds began to blow,
And Old Man Winter blustered in.
The ant, who had worked all summer long,
Ate the food he had collected
And survived the winter.
But the grasshopper,
Who had played all summer long,
Ran out of food and died miserably.

You must not take this story lightly.
You must not consider it a mere metaphor.
It reveals the truth about life.
What you have accumulated through hard work
Is not really food,
But the treasures you have stored in heaven.

In each lifetime a person lives,

They gain a certain amount of treasure.

This treasure will be stored up in heaven.

Some people will accumulate mountains of treasure

Through tens or hundreds of reincarnations,

While others will diminish their treasure

Each time they reincarnate.

In this way, your circumstances unfold

In proportion to your efforts.

This is exactly how the Mercy of Buddha is realized.

Live Your Own Life to the Fullest

Do not envy others needlessly.

You must not let jealousy cloud your mind

Just because someone was born into

A good family by luck,

Because their parents happen to be

Outstanding people,

Because they were coincidentally born in a big city,

Because their siblings have excellent careers,

Or because they have an incredibly beautiful physique.

All people have their own histories

And have worked to build themselves up

Into what and who they are.

What you see in them

Are the result of the efforts they made.

You cannot live another person's life.

You must live your own life.

What you must all keep in mind
Is not to live someone else's life under your name,
But to live out your life under your own name.
No one else can live your life for you.
So, treasure your own life.
You must treasure your life
As you would treasure your own name.

How much happier can you be
By exchanging your life with another person's?
Every person has their own
Worries and sufferings.
When you look at others,
You are only seeing their happiness
And not their worries and sufferings.
That is why you become deluded.
Do not focus only on the happiness of others
And compare it against your misery.

No matter how little you think of yourself,

There will be people who think highly of you.

So remember that, in this way,

People see everything relative to themselves.

Reap the Best Fruit Possible

Next, this is what I wish to tell you.

Among you all, some of you have lived in suffering,

Devastated by your given circumstances

And through experiencing failures many times.

Among those people,

Some of you have awakened to the Truth

Through your sufferings

And are now striving to somehow begin a good life.

But even so,

Those who repeatedly experienced failures

Have a tendency to embellish themselves

With vanity.

They decorate their miserable past with lies

Or exaggerate it to gain the sympathy of others.

However, I say unto all of you.
There is much worth in reflecting on the past.
It contains many lessons you can learn from
To live your life from now on.
Nonetheless, you must not dwell
Too long on your past,
Nor should you believe it to be who you are.
Your lives start anew each day.
You are living new lives each and every day.
You may forget this and dwell on your past,
But that is not how you should be.

Even among people who live honestly,
Some of them go suddenly quiet
And some become overly talkative
As if to hide their wounds
When it comes to the topic of their past failures.
However, this is what I think.

Rather than simply hiding old wounds,

It is more important to heal them.

Do not try to hide your wounds from others.

Nor should you embellish your wounds

And publicize them.

What is important is that you heal those wounds.

The way to heal your wounds

Is to love your life enough.

Love your life enough,

And from it, bear wonderful fruit.

This is what is important.

Let us say that

A vast apple orchard spreads before us.

In this orchard are taller trees

That have stood for decades,

As well as young trees

That are only several years old.

In general, the young trees are short

Whereas the old ones are tall.

And the amount of fruit that each tree can bear

Depends on how tall it is.

Even so, what matters is not

How many apples each tree bears.

The amount of fruit it bears is not so important.

The tree may be short,

But what matters is

That it does its best to bear abundant apples.

And, it is not enough to simply bear them.

Each tree must make its apples

The sweetest and juiciest.

It must strive to bear apples

That have a wonderful aroma

And a mellow taste—

Apples that are loved by many people.

By continuing to make efforts in the present,

These small trees will eventually grow into
Mighty trees, decades later.
They will bear wonderful fruit
Both in quantity and quality.
It is the sincere effort of the trees in their youth
That brings such rewards.

All of you,
Do not desire to live another tree's life.
Another tree may be growing on a land
Where it can better absorb water,
Or where the soil is richer.
However, if you have taken root,
You cannot move elsewhere.
You must do all you can
To accomplish your best work
Right where you are.
You must not allow your mind

To be affected by looking at other trees.
To bear the best fruit possible
In the environment you are in
Is a necessary step for you
To find true happiness.

The Joy in Receiving No Reward

I have shared with you the parable of the apples.

Again, deeply savor these words in your mind.

Life may be similar to how these apple trees

Make delicious apples for people to enjoy.

The farmer who grew those apples

May receive money in return for his work,

But the trees that actually bore those apples

Receive nothing.

Not even a single coin.

Not even a single reward.

No one offers the trees

Any words of appreciation such as,

"Good job bearing those apples."

Even so, the trees continue living their lives.

The trees know

That as long as they live as apple trees,

Their joy indeed lies
In bearing bundles of delicious apples
Year after year.
They will not stop bearing fruit in the next season
Simply because no one praised them.
They continue to strive day by day
To bear the best apples they can,
Even if they are eaten by insects,
Blown about by the wind,
Or battered by a storm.

Therefore, let me say unto all of you.
Do not say,
"No one praises me
Even though I'm doing my best."
Even apple trees do not seek to be praised.
Not to mention that all of you, human beings,
Are greater than apple trees.

With that being so,

Do not seek praise from others.

Do not seek rewards from others.

Fulfill your mission,

Regardless of whether or not you are recognized.

Just as apple trees bear fruit

At the right time every year,

You must also harvest the fruit you have borne,

Year after year,

To accomplish your mission as human beings.

Even apple trees bear bundles of fruit

At least once a year.

With that being so,

All of you humans, who are great beings,

Must definitely bear fruit year after year.

Should your fruit be plucked away

And eaten by others

Without earning you a single penny,
Make the joy of others your own regardless.
When you see them eat your fruits with joy,
Make that your own joy.
Know that true joy can be felt through
Receiving no reward.
How many fruits did you bear this year
That were able to make others happy?
Your answer to this question will tell you
Whether or not you are an outstanding tree.

The Joy of Buddha

Listen well to my words.

In this third dimensional world,

All of you are apt to inevitably suffer from

Low self-esteem.

And, you will start to seek the words of others.

You will start to seek appreciation from others.

You will start to seek advice from others.

Without them, you will feel that

Your life is worthless and empty.

There are even people who,

Despite getting praised by many people,

Lose all hope after receiving just a single criticism.

But I say unto all of you.

As long as you are living

Sincerely, truthfully, and honestly,

Buddha is always watching over you.

People in this world may not appreciate you,

But Buddha will never overlook you.

Buddha is gazing upon your acts of love.

Buddha is gazing upon your thoughts of love.

How much fruit did you bear?

How many people did you bring happiness to?

To Buddha, the answers to these questions

Are as plain as day,

And they will never be mistaken.

You must all believe this truth.

Even if the people in this world fail to recognize you,

There is nothing that can deceive the eyes of

The Primordial Buddha of the Great Universe

And the eyes of Buddha,

Who has been sent to earth

By the Primordial Buddha.

Do not rejoice in your own joy.
Believe that your joy will truly be joy
Only when Buddha savors that joy.
Make Buddha's joy your own.
What kinds of thoughts and deeds
Will bring out the joy in Buddha?
Think about this.

Yes, the Heart of Buddha is filled
With the desire to bring happiness
To all people on earth.
Then, is it not the mission of Buddha's disciples,
Who are born on this earth,
To faithfully carry out the Will of Buddha?
Your joy lies in this and this alone.

You must not be outdone by
Apple trees, peach trees, or grape vines.

Do not be outdone by those trees

That bear bundles of fruit year in and year out,

Never being praised and never complaining.

You are all greater than those trees.

Your mission will not end

Until the hearts of all people of this world

Are overflowing with joy.

The True Desire of Buddha's Disciples

Many people are still starving

In this age of plenty,

Where the world has abundant food.

However, it is particularly in this age

That many people are truly starving and suffering.

Their minds are what is starving.

It is their minds and souls

That are seeking food.

People are seeking nourishment for their souls.

There is no end to the number of people

Who are spiritually starving to death.

There is a shortage of food for the soul.

There is still a lack of food for the mind

To feed the entire population of Earth.

Therefore, all of you, as disciples of Buddha,

Must work hard day and night

To produce and deliver food for the soul,
Food for the mind.
There is no end to this work.

But blessed are they,
Who can push forward with this work,
When Buddha is on earth.
They are like travelers, walking at high noon,
Who never stray from their path.
They, who walk at high noon,
Will surely reach their destinations.
However, they who walk in the darkness
Will eventually slip and fall from the path
Into the steep valley.
Be proud about having awakened to the truth
And to be living as a person of truth
When the Light is on earth.
That is when your true desire

As disciples of Buddha will be fulfilled.

All of you,
Live honestly as a person of truth in this world.
Live for the wonderful day
When you all join hands
And rejoice together again.
Until then, let your name be hidden
And live out your life for love.

CHAPTER THREE

Imperishable Power

Diligent Efforts

All of you, my disciples,

I may be expecting too many things from you.

You may be overwhelmed

By the weight of my expectations.

You may also be wondering,

Just how far you will be able to

Carry out the resolution of

Making diligent efforts for infinity.

However, I say unto you all.

Your true power

Is not as weak as you imagine.

You all possess

A power that is extraordinarily strong.

You must not forget this.

Even taking this lifetime alone,

All things that you learn from it

Will add to your power.

Even the muscles you built

Doing sports in this lifetime will not go to waste.

Thus, if all that you gain in this life alone

Also adds to your power,

Then the power that you have gained

From the several reincarnations,

The tens of reincarnations,

Or the hundreds of reincarnations

That you have lived and trained with me

Should be incomparable

To any ordinary person.

That is how long of a time

You spent training as disciples of Buddha.

You have been making efforts steadily and tirelessly

With indomitable resolve under the motto,

"Make tomorrow better than today,

And the day after even better."
So I cannot imagine that someone like this
Can have minds that waver so easily
Or fall back in their discipline so easily.
Master and his disciples are joined
By a deep, deep bond at heart.
This bond is very difficult to cut off.

I have preached unto you,
Thousands and tens of thousands of Teachings.
These Teachings are of course precious.
But I have told you many times
About the efforts I accumulated
When forming those Teachings
And taught you to learn from it.
I have taught you time and time again,
To observe the way I made efforts and to follow me.
If I, the Master,

Were an absolutely exceptional being

And were holy without needing any training,

Then all of you, my disciples,

May feel helpless and give up on your discipline.

However, even I, the Master,

Have diligently made efforts

Every time I was born.

For a Master to stay a Master,

It is only natural that

He makes far more diligent efforts

Than his disciples.

As you observed me from behind,

You must have thought,

"If I make efforts like the Master,

I, too, might be able to reach

A state of enlightenment like his."

Yes, indeed.

I have taught you all, time and time again,

That the power of Buddha-nature

Resides equally in all human beings.

Having Buddha-nature means

You have the same nature as Buddha in you.

If, although having the same nature as Buddha,

You have not yet reached the same state as Him,

It is because you have not made enough efforts

In your past lives as well as in your current life.

If so, there is nothing you can do

By talking about the past.

The only thing you can do is

To start accumulating diligent efforts

From today onward, from this very moment.

First, let me see you making efforts.

Show me how diligent you are.

The Greatest Delight in Life

In my memories, there remain
The feelings I had when I preached the Laws
In many different countries
Several, tens, and hundreds of reincarnations ago.
Each time, your looks varied
But you were always my disciples.
You were always near me
Protecting and following me.

In some of those ages,
There were countless people who
Would even lay down their lives without hesitation
To learn the Laws that I taught.
Many people vowed to
Never give up seeking the Truth,
Even if they were to be eaten by a tiger.

Some seekers of the Truth

Were so desperate to learn the Teachings

That they wanted to record them somewhere

Even if it meant flaying their own skin.

In this way,

All of the past seekers of the Truth

Have made devout efforts

Even if it meant putting their lives at risk.

This is the spirit of diligent effort.

It is something that you stake your life for.

What does it mean to stake your life for something?

It means to know the value

Of what you are seeking;

It means to know its true worth.

To know this is the greatest delight in life.

In this world, aside from Buddha's Truth,

There are various academic studies to pursue.

You will experience all kinds of joy
Through each of those studies.
However, the joy of studying Buddha's Truth
Is irreplaceable.
Your soul will tremble in delight,
And you will dance in excitement as if on air.
This is how much joy you must find.
O, how wonderful it is to be taught
The secrets of the Great Universe
And the secrets of humankind.
O, the joy you feel in the moment
You truly believe that
There is a world beyond this one.
No thrones or noble titles of this world
Can replace this joy.
No matter how many times I say this,
I cannot stress this fact to you enough.
This is indeed true.

Can you understand how splendid it is

To choose one book of Truth

Over wearing a crown in pure gold?

It is the greatest delight

A human being can ever savor.

The Work of the Sangha

I was born into this world,

Attained the enlightenment of Buddha,

And began preaching the Laws.

Now, look at the number of books of Buddha's Truth

I have published since.

It is a Gold Mine.

The Gold Mine is right here,

Yet many people do not notice it.

They have eyes but do not see.

They have ears but do not hear.

They have hands but do not feel.

O, how foolish they are.

Now, in this age, heaven has poured down

The bountiful gold of Buddha's Truth onto earth,

And people can obtain it everywhere.

Yet, people do not realize this.

If hundreds of millions,

Or even billions of people living on earth

Depart this world without knowing

A single phrase of Buddha's Truth,

That will leave me with unbearable sadness.

Having been born as Buddha on earth

And having been preaching the Teachings,

If I fail to share even a single phrase of

Buddha's Truth to people living in the same age,

Then the sadness will be deeper than the ocean.

All of you, my disciples,

That is the work of the Sangha.

All of you have already learned

That to study Buddha's Truth,

You must devote yourself to the Three Treasures,

Which are Buddha, Dharma, and Sangha.

Buddha is the Buddha incarnate on earth.

Dharma is the Teachings preached by Buddha.

And Sangha is the group of disciples on earth

That is striving to spread Buddha's Truth.

An overwhelming amount of treasure

Is poured down from heaven

And has formed a mountain.

But if the disciples allow the people of this age

To leave this world without informing them

Even a single phrase of Buddha's Truth,

Then I must say,

The Sangha has failed to fulfill its mission.

The True Meaning of Missionary Work

All of you, my disciples,

You must realize the significance of your mission.

It seems you think that missionary work

Is a peculiar activity.

You seem to be under the illusion

That it is something strange and very difficult

To be accomplished in today's world.

However, I say unto you,

Once people understand

The true meaning of missionary work,

They will not be able to deny its greatness.

Who would get angry

If someone puts a diamond in their pocket?

Would a woman get upset

If someone puts a pearl necklace on her
And tells her, "This is for you"?
Would a person get furious
If someone gives them a sapphire ring
And says, "Please wear this"?
Of course, not.
This does not only apply to adults.
Would children throw a tantrum
If someone gives them textbooks or study guides
And tells them, "Here, use these to study"?
They would surely think, "Oh, what a precious gift"
And use them to study hard.
This is how things are.
Because the Teachings have true worth,
The very act of sharing them with others
Comes with great virtue and merit.

Those who refuse the Teachings or the Laws
That they are offered
Are like people who refuse to have
Three meals a day, and just starve to death.
But to tell you the truth,
Even if humans refuse to have meals
And end up losing their physical lives,
Their eternal lives will never perish.
However, if they did not learn Buddha's Truth,
These souls may be put to eternal death.
In other words,
When souls live without knowing Buddha's Truth,
That is the same as denying their true existence
As children of Buddha.

Behold,
The cemeteries that dot the landscapes
Of the towns and villages on earth.

There stand headstones covered in moss.
Would you not be terribly sad
If you saw dead spirits
Clinging pitifully to those headstones,
Believing that those stones are where they belong?
Would you not be unbearably sad
If this were the state of your ancestors
Or yourselves in the afterlife?
This is the consequence of
Not knowing the meaning of life and death.
What is life?
What is death?
What is the eternity of the soul?
And what does it mean to be a child of Buddha?
If you live without knowing
The answers to these questions,
Your soul will eventually die.
If you do not know

The way to make full use of your life
And do not know the meaning of it,
Then you are as good as dead.

Therefore, the deed of offering the Laws to people
Is more precious than feeding the hungry.
It is of more value
Than providing the naked with clothes
Or offering a night's stay to the homeless.
This is what it means to offer the Laws,
To share the Teachings,
And to spread the Truth.
This action, in itself, is the absolute good.

If countless people around you
Are starving to death,
You would give them whatever little food you have
So that they can survive another day.

And, if countless people are dying of thirst,
You would lower the bucket
To draw water from the well
And rush to give them water
With the limited amount of energy you have.
You would run to your very last breath
To deliver their final sip of water
Before they die.
These are all natural courses of action
As a human being.
How, then, can you pretend to be blind
When this world is overflowing with people
Whose souls are on the verge of death?
That does not accord with the Heart of Buddha.

You may all feel as though
You are battling against others.
However, that is not really true.

You are battling against yourselves.

You are battling against your vanity.

You are battling against your embarrassment.

You are battling against your shame.

You are battling against your laziness.

You are battling against your vanity

And concern for worldly reputation.

You are battling against your petty pride.

You must thoroughly battle against

All of these symbols of weakness found within you.

The Primary Vow of Buddha

Spread Buddha's Teachings
To every corner of this world
While Buddha is still on earth.
This is the Sangha's mission.
All of you, my disciples,
This is your only mission.
That is everything.
Only when you are doing the work
Of conveying the Laws
Will your enlightenment truly heighten.
You are all my disciples,
So you must strive to become bodhisattvas.
You must all become bodhisattvas.
The most important work of bodhisattvas
Is to offer the Laws to people.
This is the most precious form of "love that gives."

You all desire to become bodhisattvas.

Rather, you are bodhisattvas in essence,

So I tell you, fulfill the primary vow.

Fulfill the Will of Buddha.

Fulfill the Desire of Buddha.

Buddha has only one desire.

It is to save all humankind.

Buddha wishes for all people

Who have come together

Through their connection to Buddha

To learn all of Buddha's Truth.

He wants to deliver to each and every person

Mountains of treasure or dishes of feast.

This is the primary vow of Buddha.

To carry out this vow

Is the greatest mission of Buddha's disciples.

Besides this, there are many other things

That you must accomplish as disciples.

These are called secondary vows.

A secondary vow may be, for example,

To become a politician,

A skillful doctor,

A scholar,

Or an artist.

You may wish to fulfill

Your own mission in life

And contribute to humankind.

However, these are nothing more

Than just secondary vows.

There is only one primary vow.

It is to spread the Teachings taught by Buddha

And to have the people,

Who have connected with Buddha's Truth,

Study all of the Teachings.

Then, they will be able to create Buddha Land Utopia

By way of this earthly world.

Yes, here, too, lies the Will of Buddha.

Long ago, the earth was filled with light.

The world beyond this one, also,

Was brimming with light and in harmony.

However, through the repeated cycles of

Soul training in this world,

Humans gradually forgot

The true nature of their souls.

People grew egotistic while living in this world

And began to oppress others

As they sought personal glory.

This is how humankind

Gave birth to desires unique to this earthly world.

The rise of worldly desires

Was the beginning of the fall of humankind.

Some gave in to their desires,

Expanded their ego, gained more power,

And dragged many people into suffering.

Others spread negative emotions out of misery

Because they could not fulfill their desires,

And sunk into the abyss.

Among the people in this earthly world,

Some endlessly sought to fulfill their worldly desires

And some others died in suffering

Because they were unable to fulfill their worldly desires.

In this way, the existence of this earthly world

Became the trigger that created hell.

Therefore, we must start over from the beginning

And use this earthly world

To establish Buddha Land instead.

Humans are the ones who created hell,

So humans must be the ones to dissolve hell
Through their own thoughts and actions.
This is a noble duty.

Prescription for the Soul

Then, what should you do?

First is to spread Buddha's Truth.

Next is to have people learn all of Buddha's Truth.

In other words,

Buddha's Truth is a way for the soul to stay healthy.

To many of the people with ailing souls, it teaches,

"If you live by this prescription,

Your soul will recover from its illness."

That is why the Truth is so valuable.

"Why?" you may all ask.

You may wonder,

"If humans live in the land created by Buddha,

Why do so many souls get ill?"

But I say unto you,

In all the hundreds and thousands of times

You were born on earth,

Not once was your soul born

Into the same environment.

The environment your soul trains in

Has been different in every life.

And to figure out how to live

In different environments

Gives you a new kind of soul training.

And because you undergo new soul training,

Mistakes are bound to happen.

If, to avoid making mistakes,

Your souls were reincarnated

Into exactly the same environment as your past,

You would certainly not make any mistakes.

But at the same time,

There would be no progress.

Then, humankind would fall into stagnation.

Buddha abandoned stagnation and chose progress.
Because He chose progress,
Humans started to undergo soul training
In different environments.
And because of this, souls who had difficulty
Adapting to their new environments
Began to fail in their soul training, one after another.
This is why Buddha is telling these souls,
"Do not forget your starting point,"
"Do not forget the true nature of your mind,"
And is providing them with prescriptions.
To deliver these prescriptions
To patients who need them
Is indeed your mission.

Listen well.
You can never have done enough of this mission.
You can never do too much in fulfilling it.

There are no limits to
How deeply and extensively
You will fulfill the mission.

The Path of Giving Back

Even so, the strongest desire of the Sangha
Is to fulfill the primary vow of Buddha
While His life is still on earth.
The most important path as Buddha's disciples
Is to respond to and realize Buddha's Wish
While He is here on earth.

Disciples must walk the path of giving back.
The path of giving back
Is to have gratitude to Buddha
For having given Buddha's Truth to humans.
Your gratitude to Buddha
For being taught Buddha's Truth
And being shown the right path to live
Will manifest as acts of giving back.
And to truly give back to Buddha,

You must spread Buddha's Teachings
To every corner of the world.
Never forget this.

Behold, look up.
Look around you, look upon the world,
Look at the people from all walks of life.
Alas, there are people here and there,
Who live in complete ignorance of Buddha's Truth.
O, how wonderful this world would be,
If all of these people built their lives
Upon Buddha's Truth.
Each person would of course
Be capable of solving the problems of their mind
On their own.
But if they continue making progress
In their spiritual discipline
And become capable of taking on the role of teacher,

They can provide a great amount
Of advice for living life
To people who are taking their first steps
On the path of learning.
Thus, when you live your life wonderfully,
And if your wonderful life
Educates and leads many people,
That would prove that
The Laws are truly spreading.

Bodhisattvas of the Earth

All of you, my disciples,

As I said in the beginning,

You must not think that this work is difficult.

You have been given an imperishable power.

This power springs from the truth that,

First,

You are all children of Buddha,

And second,

You have lived and studied the Truth

As Buddha's disciples

For tens, hundreds, thousands,

And tens of thousands of reincarnations.

As Buddha's children,

You have continuously studied Buddha's Teachings.

This means that

The power that you possess is almost infinite.

Enjoy this power that springs forth.

Rejoice in this wisdom that bursts forth.

Honor this power of love that gushes out endlessly.

When you engrave the sacred mission

Into your hearts

And are strongly determined to fulfill your mission,

Each of you will become

A Bodhisattva of the Earth.

Bodhisattvas of the Earth will appear,

One after the other,

As if they have emerged from the land.

I wish to see this happening with my own eyes;

I wish to see many Bodhisattvas of the Earth

Emerge on all lands, here and there.

I wish to see the lands

Being filled with countless bodhisattvas

Accomplishing great work.

Is this not how
Buddha Land will be established on earth?

Your mission is to establish Buddha Land.
Buddha Land must be established.
It is unacceptable not to establish it.
So, from this day forward,
You shall never slack off on your journey.
Cherish every moment, every step,
And strive to create Buddha Land on earth.
That is when Buddha's disciples will shine the most.

From now on,
Rid yourselves of all excuses
And all wrong thoughts,
And wholeheartedly walk this path, on and on.

CHAPTER FOUR

The Time to Make a Leap

A Time of Miracles

Now,

I shall talk about something very important for you.

It is about something that you absolutely need to know

For your soul to leap to a whole new level.

There are times when you may feel

Bored of living ordinary lives every day.

If this is you, I want to say,

Life is not as boring as you may think.

Life is not only made up of

Simple, ordinary days as you may believe.

When you were young,

You may have heard that people go through

Various events in life

And you had a feeling that

You, too, will go through them one day.

You were right.

It is quite possible

For people who appeared to be living ordinary lives

To one day suddenly transform into

A completely different person.

Some of you might think,

"That's ridiculous.

I'm the last person who could change like that."

But I would like you to stop for a moment

And listen closely to what I say.

At the very least,

You should be holding this book that I wrote

In your hands and reading it now.

The act of picking up and reading this book

That I wrote

Is an extraordinary event in itself.

It is a significant event that will completely shift you

From who you are now to a new you.

In the long history of humankind,

This age we are living in now is of the utmost importance.

I have told you this time and time again,

Yet, many of you still do not realize

The importance of it.

This is because you still have not managed

To step out of being ordinary.

But I say unto you.

You must realize that

To be born in the same age as the rebirth of Buddha

And to encounter His Teachings is extraordinary in itself.

Furthermore, if your life changes completely

After encountering Buddha's Teachings,
Then that is indeed, a moment of miracle.

Throughout the history of humankind,
Many great tathagatas were born on earth
With physical bodies
And accomplished very sacred work.
You can all probably imagine quite easily that
As these tathagatas strived to complete
Their sacred mission,
Many souls were enveloped in light that
They had never experienced before.
Human beings reincarnate time and time again,
Each time to take on new soul training.
And, when you learn the teachings of great tathagatas
At the time of their descent,
Your soul will make a great leap

In its spiritual progress.
I am not exaggerating when I say that
One lifetime of soul training
In the presence of a great tathagata
Is worth ten ordinary lifetimes of soul training.
In fact, some of you will go through soul training
That will be worth even more than that.

Yes, you will,
Because a light that is like the sunlight
Will shine upon you,
Unlock your closed heart and make its way into it.
It will cast away every shadow
And shed light onto every corner of your mind.
At that time,
Your soul will surely remember that nostalgic sensation
You had long forgotten.

All of you,
You look upon the blind and sympathize with them.
You look upon the deaf and sympathize with them.
You look upon those who cannot smell
And sympathize with them.
You look upon those with crippled legs
And feel sorry for them.
You look upon those with crippled hands
And feel sorry for them.
Yet, you do not feel any inconvenience
When your soul's eyes are closed,
Your soul's ears are plugged,
Your soul's nose cannot smell,
Your soul's mouth cannot eat,
Your soul's hands are bound
And your soul's feet are crippled.
That is because you have been living in oblivion
For a long, long time.

However, the moment you discover the truth,
You will have no choice but to change yourselves.

True Equality and Freedom

Humans are truly mystical beings.
A mature human soul enters the mother's womb
And endures months of soul training in darkness.
Then, by the time the soul is born as a baby,
It will have lost all of its past memories.
All souls start their lives
On an equal footing with a clean slate.
Some may say that this makes no sense.
Some people might argue that,
Since every soul progresses at a different speed,
It is not fair for everyone to start from nothing.
This is understandable.

However, ponder this:
You often hear about equality and freedom,
But what do they truly mean?

What is true equality?

The only equality that humans are bestowed is that

All souls, regardless of their spiritual levels,

Enter a mother's womb,

And when they are born as babies

They start with a blank slate with

No recollection of all their past lives.

Then, what is true freedom?

It is that every person is entrusted with

The responsibility of building their own reputation

Through the process of

Beginning their lives as a baby with a blank slate,

Expressing their individuality,

Developing their own character

Through their thoughts and deeds,

And then working in society.

These are the true meanings of equality and freedom.

Therefore, you must respect this fact
And be in awe of it at the same time.
It is a precious opportunity to be able to begin
This life anew
And to begin on equal footing with others,
Regardless of how you lived in the past.
Rejoice in this opportunity
With which Buddha has blessed you.

For example,
If a person is born with the awareness of a tathagata,
Or the mind of a tathagata,
He will accomplish even more powerful work.
Likewise, if a person who is born
With a mediocre level of enlightenment
Continues to live with that same awareness,
Then, the spiritual level between the two souls
Would widen even more.

In actual fact, they begin their life
On the same starting line.
They will not see themselves as different people,
But as equal human beings.
As they undergo their soul training
And compete with each other
To strive toward improvement,
They will begin to notice
How differently their souls shine
And will ask themselves why there is a difference.
A great opportunity lies in this.

Try to imagine
How excited the souls in heaven are
Before they are born into this world.
How joyful and happy they are.
These souls are in utmost delight.
They are given an opportunity to be reborn

With a completely blank slate, once again.
How great their joy is.
Their joy is as though they can soar into the sky.
Oh, how precious it is to be able to think,
"All right, I will make a clean break with my past
And start over once more."

However, as each person progresses in their cultivation,
They will do so in the direction that accords to
The tendency of their soul.
Some people will have a strong sense of responsibility,
Have control over their minds,
And find joy in guiding others,
Whereas others will live their lives
Without ever feeling an ounce of shame
Even when they have inflicted pain on others.
This is a major crossroads for the soul.

Nonetheless, this is what I think.

Wouldn't you agree that

By knowing the true equality and freedom that

I have described,

You can design or even redesign your life?

Wouldn't you agree that

This is when you are given a new chance?

If the time you were born into this world as a baby

Is your first chance,

Your second chance would be

The time when you discover Buddha's Truth

And are able to redesign your life.

This is exactly the time for your soul to make a leap.

The Root of the Soul

Now, then,

When you discover Buddha's Truth,

Making your second leap in life,

Achieving your second birth in life,

What should you keep in mind?

The first thing you must do

Is to look back on your past.

How have you lived so far?

You must re-evaluate your life up to this point.

Trace back the paths you took in your life

And reflect carefully on each of them, one by one.

Blessed are the ones

Who, during such reflection,

Remember Buddha's Truth well

And practice self-reflection based on it.

What should you have thought?

What should you *not* have thought?

What should you have done?

What should you *not* have done?

The answers are clear under the Sun,

The Sun of Buddha's Truth.

At that time,

If you discover that you had the wrong thoughts

Or did wrong to others,

You should reflect deeply and thoroughly on them.

However, reflection on your thoughts and deeds

Is not all there is.

There is more to self-reflection.

Your reflection must delve much deeper.

You must look into and verify

What kind of soul you have.

For every thought you have and action you take,

There is a root cause

At the depth of your soul and mind.

You must all look back on the thoughts and deeds

That you had up to this day,

And think about what kind of root

Your soul stems from.

Contemplate this deeply and thoroughly.

Then, you will clearly understand

The soul training you must do in this lifetime.

If you are lazy and do not make this effort

And instead, simply reflect on your bad thoughts

Or vow never to repeat your bad deeds,

That is far from enough.

If you have such a tendency at the root of your soul,

Then you will eventually fall back into

Doing the same thing as time passes.

When we think about it,
Every soul has its own tendency
That is very difficult to change.
Just as a speeding bullet train cannot immediately stop
The moment you apply the emergency brakes,
The law of inertia also governs
The tendencies of your soul.
So even if you suddenly apply
The emergency brakes to stop
Or try to suddenly steer to the left or right,
It will be difficult.

So, I say unto all of you.
Blessed are those of you
Who have found what lies at the root of your soul
Relatively early in your lives.
For the remainder of your lives,

Work hard to gradually change
The tendencies of your souls, little by little.

Search Out the Gold Coin

On the other hand,
Those who discover the nature of their souls
In their twilight years
Must know that they have challenging work
Waiting for them.
You would be frantic
If you had to search for a gold coin at dusk.
No matter how hard you search for a gold coin
During sunset,
Sometimes it cannot be found.
In due time, the sun goes down completely.
At times like this, light a torch.
When the torch casts a light,
The gold coin will definitely reflect the light
And show you its whereabouts
Even if it is covered in grass.

Likewise,

Those who have discovered Buddha's Truth

For the first time

In their twilight years

Should hold the Truth up high, as they would a torch.

This means that, from that point on,

They should be determined to

Put all their life and energy into

Reaching higher and higher for Buddha's Truth

With high aspirations.

Fortunately, you have all accumulated

Various experiences that can help you.

You have knowledge as well.

So, use your experiences and knowledge

As a platform from which

To climb to great heights.

Climb the tower.

From the top of the tower,
Raise the torch of Buddha's Truth up high.
When you do,
You will find the gold coin that you had lost.
The gold coin is your good nature,
The Buddha-nature within you.
It is your diamond-like mind.
It is your conscience.
You must search for and find it.
And, if the gold coin is dirty,
You must clean it immediately.
This is important.

Now, once you find your gold coin,
You must cherish it.
The gold coin you found at dusk is worth a fortune.
Do not waste it.
Spend it on what is truly important.

Spend it on things that will truly benefit the world.

That is when you will be acknowledged to be genuine

As a person who learns Buddha's Truth.

The moment you discover Buddha's Truth,

Whenever that may be,

Your mind will change,

Your life will change.

In fact, they will inevitably change.

Thus, you must never forget the moment

You took this book in your hands and read it.

It is now time for your soul to make a great leap.

Now that you have heard my Teachings,

You must not corrupt your soul.

All souls are to just aim for higher growth.

The Path of Right Thought

And, one of the ways for souls to grow
Is through reflective meditation.

In the past, I taught you the Eightfold Path.
It is the eight right paths.
View rightly.
Think rightly.
Speak rightly.
Act rightly.
Live rightly.
Make efforts rightly.
Use your will rightly.
And meditate rightly.
If you have awakened to Buddha's Truth
Somewhere along your life,
These eight right paths are

Indeed the sacred practice for building your character
Into something as true as a gem.

If I had to pick out one path in the Eightfold Path
That is of particular importance,
It would be to think rightly.
Everything comes down to this single point.

Look around you.
Look at the mindset
Of the people who surround you.
Look at their states of mind.
How disgraceful are the things
They think about all day long!
Alas, how big is the number of people
Who are more or less thinking of nothing!
I must say that the lives of people
Who live thinking of nothing

Are inferior to that of an insect.

Even insects think hard as they search

For their own food.

They choose their course

And try to avoid anything that might attack them.

That is how they survive.

Therefore, we can say

That people who live thoughtlessly

Are living lives that are worth less than

The life of an insect.

The greatest value in being born as a human

And living as a human

Comes down to the ability to think.

To put it another way,

To think rightly means to correct your thoughts.

Your qualities as a human

All depend on the content of your thoughts.

If you could see the minds of others
And see what is inside them
As if they were a clear glass box,
How would you feel?
You would most likely be shocked.
What would you do
If you had a chalkboard hung around your neck
And all of your thoughts appeared on it,
All written in chalk?
You would not be able to walk down the street
Or look another person in the eyes
Because all of the thoughts you have
Would be displayed in writing for everyone to see.

Then, what should you do?
There are two basic and important things.
First, think about things
That you will not mind others seeing,

Namely, thoughts that are in line with Buddha's Truth.
Second, should you think about things
That are against the Truth,
Correct them immediately.
Correct them straightaway, thinking to yourself,
"I've had wrong thoughts.
Those were absolutely shameful thoughts
In light of my conscience."
If you do this, your soul will be cleansed
And impurities will be removed.

As you explore the right thoughts in this way,
Your soul will gradually gain more and more power.
Great people are those who have great thoughts.
This is an important point.

Washing the Fabric of Your Soul

Now, I will take this opportunity

To explain further to you in simple words.

Perhaps you think of having great thoughts

As having extraordinary thoughts,

As having complex ideas,

Or as having thoughts that no one else would think of.

But I say unto you,

It is indeed important to have thoughts

That are extraordinary in content

And which other people would not think of,

But there is a prerequisite that you must fulfill first.

That is, no matter how great your thoughts may be,

Unless you have a pure mind,

They will all be in vain.

The most important thing for the human soul
Is for its foundation to be kept pure.
The root of the soul must be washed clean
And be free of all impurities.
The soul must be transparent.
The soul must be purified, first and foremost,
For if you disregard it,
Then no matter how much knowledge
You store within you,
Sadly, it will bear no fruit.
Yes, all of that knowledge
Will just be a castle built on sand.

Behold the ones who are lauded
As successful in this world
And the ones who are deemed
Incredibly knowledgeable in this world.
Are they not the ones building castles on sand?

Is their true nature as a human being, pure?
Are they selfless in their minds?
Without a mind that possesses these traits,
They may only be accumulating ideas,
Studying various subjects,
And absorbing specialized knowledge
Because they want to expand their business,
Because they want to acquire knowledge,
Or because they want to gain worldly status.
But these efforts will all be fruitless.
Sooner or later, when a gust blows,
Their castles built on sand
Will helplessly crumble.
This gust is the wind of impermanence
That comes from the other world.
Not a single person can avoid it.
It is a wind that comes
At the end of your life.

A castle built on sand will never survive the gust.
It will crumble from its very foundation.

Therefore, it is important
That you build a firm foundation
Before your soul makes a leap.
Examine your mind daily
And check to see that there is nothing evil in it.
Do you have evil thoughts lurking in your mind?
Do you have greedy thoughts?
Do you have strong thoughts of vanity?
Do you have condescending thoughts?
Do you have thoughts
That could destroy your own soul?
Examine these points about yourself.
In this way, wash the fabric of your soul every day.
Only after the fabric has been washed and dried
Can it be dyed in beautiful colors.

You can draw many pictures on a clean, white fabric.
Keep this in your hearts.

When the Soul Makes a Great Leap

I have now given many Truths unto you.

I have told you

That it is important to have the right thoughts

When developing your character.

I have told you

That to have the right thoughts means to think rightly.

I have told you

That the foundation of right thinking

Is to first purify your mind.

And to do that,

I have told you to sweep out on a daily basis,

The dust that covers your mind.

As you continue to study the Great Truth,

Or as you grasp the Great Truth and practice it in society,

A scenery that no one has ever seen

Will unfold before you.
You will be surprised to find how powerful you are.
You will wonder if that person is really you.
This is a wonderful experience.

It will be clear when your soul makes a leap
Because you will be filled with joy at that time.
Only when you feel yourself improving
Can your soul truly feel joy.
You will know that you are making a leap
As it will be reflected in the scenery you see around you.
When your soul makes a great leap,
You will see happiness in people's faces.
You will see hope in people's faces.
You will see goodness in people.
You will see the light as children of Buddha in people.
And, you will have infinite love for the fact
That you and the people around you are

All living their own unique lives.
Further, you will be filled with gratitude and light
For the food, environment, Mother Nature
And all else that have been given to you.

Savor this joy of the soul.
This is the joy that awaits you
After your soul makes a leap.
Make this joy your own.
Suffering is not all there is in the path of discipline.
True discipline is accompanied by true joy.
This joy of the soul
Will make your long journey feel lighter
And will also enable you to enjoy it.
Come walk this path together with me.

CHAPTER FIVE

The Eternal Buddha

I Am Greater Than a Savior

All of you, my disciples.
In the depth of your soul, engrave my voice,
Which you heard in the long distant past.
Two thousand six hundred years of time and space later
You are now, here, hearing it again.

You are very fortunate
To hear my voice while you are still alive on earth.
You must willfully cast all things aside
And choose to seize this blissful moment.

I am the Everlasting Buddha, the Eternal Buddha.
Through tens and hundreds of reincarnations,
I have always been
The Everlasting Buddha,

The Everlasting Master,
The Eternal Buddha.

The Eternal Buddha is, thus,
The Eternal Laws themselves.
The Eternal Laws are, thus,
The Will of the Primordial Buddha of the Universe
Expressed in the form of principles and Teachings.
You must thoroughly understand
The value of these Laws.
Never overlook a single word that I preach.
Read these words carefully
And absorb the light in each one of them.

O, you, who vowed to be my disciple
And kept the promise for eons,
By now, you must be well aware

Of the warning signs that are seen everywhere,
Calling for an age of salvation.

Listen closely to my words.
I did not come to this world as a savior.
I came to this world
As One greater than a savior.
People can naturally be saved
By the Laws that I teach
By taking them to heart and studying them well.
However, the purpose of My Teachings
Should not be reduced
To solely saving the people on earth.
They have a much greater purpose.
This universe, this very world,
Was created based upon My Words and My Teachings.

Buddha Is the Laws and Also the Teachings

Again, I say unto all of you.

I am not preaching these Teachings to you

Solely for the sake of saving your souls.

These Teachings are what govern the entire universe.

I will tell you clearly:

The past, present, and future of humankind

Are there for humans

To realize these Teachings;

They strictly existed in the past,

Before humankind,

And will still exist in the future,

After humankind.

The Laws that I preach

Existed before the birth of humankind,

And shall continue to exist

After the extinction of humankind.

You must understand

That the Teachings are Buddha Himself,

Expressed in a different form.

To read My Teachings is the same as seeing Buddha.

If you desire to know Buddha, look at My Teachings.

The Teachings are indeed

The real entity of the shapeless, formless Buddha.

Do you look up at the skies when trying to see Buddha?

Do you close your eyes when trying to see Buddha?

Do you imagine Buddha when trying to see Him?

Or do you try opening your spiritual eyes

To see Buddha?

All of these attempts will only end in vain.

Indeed, the Real Buddha is without shape or form.

The Real Buddha is beyond a spiritual being

Who takes the form of a high spirit

In the Real World beyond this world.

The Real Buddha transcends a spiritual being.

His true nature appears in His Teachings.

All of you who seek

To touch Buddha with your hands,

To see Buddha with your eyes,

Or to try to understand Buddha's size

By comparing it with your own,

Listen very carefully.

Buddha cannot be grasped

Through your five senses.

Buddha is not what you imagine Him to be.

Buddha is the Laws.

Buddha is the Teachings.

The Laws that I preach,

The Teachings that I preach,

Are indeed the real entity of Buddha.

When you studied My Teachings
You saw Buddha.
When you heard My Teachings
You heard the Voice of Buddha.
When you understood My Teachings
You understood the Will of Buddha.

I say unto you, again and again.
Buddha is shapeless and formless.
Buddha transcends a human.
What is more, Buddha transcends a spirit.
Buddha transcends the human senses.
He is the very Being
That has become the Teachings themselves
That govern the entire universe.

You are seeing Buddha Himself
Through each and every page of this book that

You hold in your hands.

If you wish to know what Buddha is,

Try to understand the Teachings that I preach

As deeply as you can.

Then, the answer to the question, "What is Buddha?"

Will become clear to you.

One Hundred Billion Years of History

O, how long ago it was.

One hundred billion years ago,

I already existed

And was about to create this Great Universe.

I designed through My Will

How the universe ought to be.

Then, I formed the Laws

Which were to run through the entire universe.

The Laws are the blood vessels and the blood itself

That flow throughout the universe.

Through these Laws,

The universe appears as one magnificent body.

One hundred billion years ago,

In the far distant past,

When I decided to create the universe

And was designing it,
This is what I thought:

All beings,
Aim to progress infinitely.
And all beings,
Do not be weak-minded.
To make you become even greater beings,
I will give you harsh trials and tribulations.
Turning iron sand into steel
Requires intense tempering by flame,
Intense tempering by water,
And intense tempering with a hammer.
And through all of this, be strong.
Be infinitely forged.
Be infinitely beautiful.
Be infinitely good.

This is what I wished.

The one hundred billion years of history that followed

Is within My Will.

Every change in history happened within My Will.

O, My children,

Who do not know the Will of the One

Who existed at the beginning.

You must throw away the value standards

You acquired in your short, few decades of finite life.

One hundred billion years ago,

There was a Will that created all of you,

And it has been nurturing all of you

To become infinitely good.

Do not forget this.

The Moment of Glory

Ah, it feels as if it was only yesterday that

This solar system was created.

The Sun was born,

And then the planets orbiting it were born.

O, all of you small beings

Living on this planet,

I am sure you cannot even begin to imagine

The joy I felt when I gave birth to each planet,

The joy I felt when I created each planet.

You will never know the delight I felt

When I created each planet

And sent living creatures down upon it.

Nevertheless, I daresay unto you.

The planet you live in

Was created with joy.

All things that live on this planet,

All animals, plants, minerals, and humankind
Were created with joy.
All things were born with joy
For the purpose of bringing Buddha's reign
Into realization.

Ah, this sacred, noble joy.
Can you not imagine
That noble moment, that magnificent beginning?
Is it so difficult to do?
Abandon your small, trivial thoughts
And become one with the Grand, Majestic Will.
You must discard your frame of mind
That you built after being born,
Raised, and having been living as human beings
And become one with the Will of Buddha
Who created the universe.
Unbind your minds,

Shed your shell called the physical body,

And become one with the Will of Buddha.

Then, the moment of glory

Will be recalled in your mind.

You will surely feel

The joy I felt when I created the solar system,

The joy I felt when I created the Earth.

The Choice of Humankind

More than 4.6 billion years have passed
Since the Earth was created,
But it feels as if it was only yesterday
In My one hundred billion years of solitude.
I am He Who holds the ultimate authority
Over all matters regarding the Earth.
Abiding by, spreading, and realizing
The Buddha's Truth that I preach
Is indeed the true way to live as a human being.

I, once again, have revealed the Laws to you.
I showed you the principles
By which to live as human beings.
Whether or not you will abide by these principles
And build a wonderful Buddha Land Utopia
Is up to you, human beings.

Should My Teachings reach people's hearts
And Buddha Land appear on earth,
You may call yourselves true children of Buddha.
However, I will also leave you a stern warning.
Should the Teachings that I preach not spread,
Not save humankind, and instead be discarded
As meaningless words in the current of time,
Humankind will no longer be allowed
To live on earth.

Will you follow My Teachings
And build Buddha Land?
Or, will you pay no heed to My Teachings
And instead leave humankind to perish?
Choose. You must choose.
It is one or the other.
Will you choose to prosper or to perish?
You must know that there is a stern side to My Will.

At times, My Teachings embody love.

At other times, they become a fierce sword.

Because parents wish for

The true growth of their children,

Sometimes, they strictly teach their children

An ideal they must attain

And demand that they realize it.

You must know this.

Again, I will say unto you.

It all depends on what you choose.

Ever since I created the Earth

And allowed humankind to live on it,

I have been teaching you,

"Based on the Laws,

Build Buddha Land and live in happiness."

I am telling you this fact once again.

It is up to you to decide

Whether to believe and act upon it, or not.

But I will be very clear about this:

Should you have no desire, make no effort,

Or see no hope in realizing Buddha Land

And instead choose to become stagnant and corrupt,

What awaits is the extinction of humankind.

Be Brave and Stand Up

Especially you, my disciples,

Who have been studying My Teachings

Over many lifetimes.

You must stop depending on your Master.

Your Master has already preached the Teachings.

It is the mission of my disciples

To spread these Teachings.

Should you fail to spread these Teachings,

That is shameful as a disciple;

That is a blunder as a disciple.

Think to yourself again.

Think once more, why you were given life this time.

If you have truly understood the words that I speak,

You must know that

There is not a moment to spare.

The Laws are the Light of Buddha,

The true nature of the Light of Buddha.

Because they are the Light of Buddha,

They will not forgive anything that goes against them.

The Light will crush and vanquish all darkness

And fulfill the Mission of Light.

I pray that you will, by no chance,

Become the darkness driven out by the Light.

Listen carefully.

The very act of neglecting your mission

Of spreading My Teachings, in itself,

Means you are supporting the forces of darkness.

Cast away all sense of embarrassment,

Fight against all apathy,

Conquer all worldly temptations,

And stand up alone, courageously.

When a brave one stands in solitude,

This person will acquire the Sacred Light.

So, be brave and stand up.

Fight against your weaknesses

And fight against all things that prevent

The Laws of Buddha from manifesting in this world.

You shall not hesitate to spread

What is of greatest worth.

O, disciples of Buddha.

Be proud that you have gathered in Buddha's Sangha.

Aim to become the supreme.

Aim to become the greatest.

Aim to become the most powerful.

It means none other than

Restoring your true self.

All things are granted life through the Will of Buddha.

When you understand this most basic fact,

You will realize the truth that

The supreme, the greatest,

And the most powerful of all

Is the Eternal Buddha Himself.

And Buddha on earth is the one who,

Through his Teachings,

Tells people about the Eternal Buddha.

Now, Here,
Is the Light of the Eternal Buddha

Go forth.

Go forth and convey My Words.

Convey the Words of the Eternal Buddha.

Convey the Eternal Truth.

Convey the Eternal Laws.

The Eternal Buddha has been reborn in the East

And is speaking now.

Convey this fact to people all over Japan.

Convey it to people all over the world.

Convey it to millions of people.

Convey it to billions of people.

Pass it down to the people of future generations.

Convey it to those in the underworld.

Tell them,

"Now is the time for you to be set free

From the prison of souls,
From the purgatory of souls."
The Light of the Eternal Buddha
Is now, here, with you.

Believe.
Look.
Listen.
And feel the power of My Words.
Grasp the meaning of My Words.
Realize that they are the Gospel of Hope.
This is where everything begins
And this is where everything ends.

When you fully believe
In the Eternal Buddha,
You, too, will truly live on
As beings with eternal life.

Afterword (original edition)

The Eternal Buddha is the Eternal Truth and the Eternal Laws.

Buddha is human and is also the Laws. He is the Laws and is also human. What is more, He is the ultimate manifestation of love that transcends regions and eras.

This book is a treasure for humankind. It is the most precious gem.

Do not let it go to waste. You must not let this mountain of diamonds go to waste. Nor should you keep it all to yourself.

Everything is here. The source of all Teachings is here. The source of all enlightenment is here.

You must know that now, the Eternal Buddha is before you, and is walking with you.

> *Ryuho Okawa*
> *Master & CEO of Happy Science Group*
> *July 1991*

Afterword (revised edition)

At times, my words are quiet and serene, and at other times, they are solemn and strike people's hearts. I believe this book has been able to convey what Buddha's sermon is like to all people.

The flow of my words becomes intense and rapid in Chapter Five, "The Eternal Buddha." It gives readers a chance to get a glimpse of the consciousness and spiritual existence at the depth of Buddha, El Cantare. However, you do not need to deeply understand it. All you need to do is get a sense of the Light that shines from the Light Body that is at the depth of Shakyamuni Buddha and Jesus Christ. Let the rest remain a mystery of the Real World.

I believe that our activities in the past decade have almost succeeded in defeating the darkness that prevailed at the end of this century. From the outside, I may have appeared extravagant at times, but on the inside, I have been accumulating serious, precise, and steady efforts every day.

Tens and hundreds of thousands of people have gathered in response to my words in this book, which I gave in 1991. I would like to give my heartfelt gratitude to these Children of Light who have laid down their lives and taken an active role in our movement as Bodhisattvas of the Earth.

Ryuho Okawa
Master & CEO of Happy Science Group
End of July, 1999

ABOUT THE AUTHOR

Founder and CEO of Happy Science Group.

Ryuho Okawa was born on July 7th 1956, in Tokushima, Japan. After graduating from the University of Tokyo with a law degree, he joined a Tokyo-based trading house. While working at its New York headquarters, he studied international finance at the Graduate Center of the City University of New York. In 1981, he attained Great Enlightenment and became aware that he is El Cantare with a mission to bring salvation to all humankind.

In 1986, he established Happy Science. It now has members in 170 countries across the world, with more than 700 branches and temples as well as 10,000 missionary houses around the world.

He has given over 3,500 lectures (of which more than 150 are in English) and published over 3,150 books (of which more than 600 are Spiritual Interview Series), many of which are translated into 42 languages. Along with *The Laws of the Sun* and *The Laws of Hell*, many of the books have become best sellers or million sellers. To date, Happy Science has produced 27 movies under his supervision. He has given the original story and concept and is also the Executive Producer. He has also composed music and written lyrics for over 450 pieces.

Moreover, he is the Founder of Happy Science University and Happy Science Academy (Junior and Senior High School), Founder and President of the Happiness Realization Party, Founder and Honorary Headmaster of Happy Science Institute of Government and Management, Founder of IRH Press Co., Ltd., and the Chairperson of NEW STAR PRODUCTION Co., Ltd. and ARI Production Co., Ltd.

BOOKS BY RYUHO OKAWA

Buddhist Title

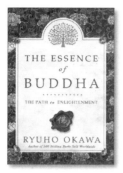

The Essence of Buddha
The Path to Enlightenment
Paperback • 208 pages • $14.95
ISBN: 978-1-942125-06-8 (Oct. 1, 2016)

The essence of Shakyamuni Buddha's original teachings of the mind are explained in simple words. Through this book, you will learn how to attain inner happiness, the wisdom to conquer ego, and to enter the path to enlightenment. It is a way of life that people in this modern age can practice to achieve lifelong self-growth.

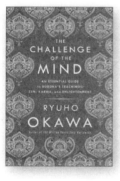

The Challenge of the Mind
An Essential Guide to Buddha's Teachings: Zen, Karma and Enlightenment
Paperback • 208 pages • $16.95
ISBN: 978-1-942125-45-7 (Nov. 15, 2018)

In this book, Ryuho Okawa explains essential Buddhist tenets and how to put them into practice. Enlightenment is not just an abstract idea but one that everyone can experience to some extent. Okawa offers a solid basis of reason and an intellectual understanding of Buddhist concepts.

The Challenge of Enlightenment
Now, Here, the New Dharma Wheel Turns
Paperback • 380 pages • $17.95
ISBN: 978-1-942125-92-1 (Dec. 20, 2022)

Buddha's teachings, a reflection of his eternal wisdom, are like a bamboo pole used to change the course of your boat in the rapid stream of the great river called life. By reading this book, your mind becomes clearer and learns to savor inner peace, and you will be empowered to make profound life improvements.

The True Eightfold Path

Guideposts for Self-Innovation

Paperback • 256 pages • $16.95

ISBN: 978-1-942125-80-8 (Mar. 30, 2021)

This book explains how we can apply the Eightfold Path, one of the main pillars of Shakyamuni Buddha's teachings, as everyday guideposts in the modern age to achieve self-innovation to live better and make positive changes in these uncertain times.

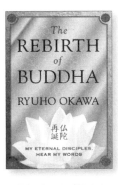

The Rebirth of Buddha

My Eternal Disciples, Hear My Words

Paperback • 280 pages • $17.95

ISBN: 978-1-942125-95-2 (Jul. 15, 2022)

These are the messages of Buddha who has returned to this modern age as promised to his eternal beloved disciples. They are in simple words and poetic style, yet contain profound messages. Once you start reading these passages, you will remember why you chose to be born in the same era as Buddha. Listen to the voices of your Eternal Master and awaken to your calling.

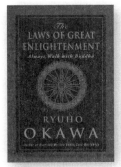

The Laws of Great Enlightenment

Always Walk with Buddha

Paperback • 232 pages • $17.95

ISBN: 978-1-942125-62-4 (Nov. 7, 2019)

Discover the power of forgiveness from Buddha's enlightenment and compassion, and the true relationship of work and enlightenment which refutes the instant enlightenment advocated in some Zen schools. In addition, the author reveals his own experience when he attained the Great Enlightenment on March 23, 1981.

El Cantare Trilogy

The Laws Series is an annual volume of books that are comprised of Ryuho Okawa's lectures that function as universal guidance to all people. They are of various topics that were given in accordance with the changes that each year brings. *The Laws of the Sun*, the first publication of the Laws Series, ranked in the annual best-selling list in Japan in 1994. Since then, the Laws Series' titles have ranked in the annual best-selling list every year for more than two decades, setting socio-cultural trends in Japan and around the world. The first three Laws Series are *The Laws of the Sun*, *The Golden Laws*, and *The Laws of Eternity*.

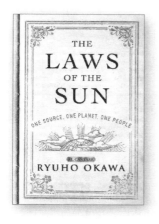

The Laws of the Sun

One Source, One Planet, One People

Paperback • 288 pages • $15.95
ISBN: 978-1-942125-43-3 (Oct. 25, 2018)

IMAGINE IF YOU COULD ASK GOD why He created this world and about the spiritual laws He used to shape us and everything around us. If we could understand His designs and intentions, we could discover what our goals in life should be and whether our actions move us closer to those goals or farther away.

At a young age, a spiritual calling prompted Ryuho Okawa to outline what he innately understood to be universal truths for all humankind. In *The Laws of the Sun*, Okawa outlines these laws of the universe and provides a road map for living one's life with greater purpose and meaning. In this powerful book, Ryuho Okawa reveals the transcendent nature of consciousness and the secrets of the multidimensional universe as well as the meaning of humans that exist within it. By understanding the different stages of love and following the Buddhist Eightfold Path, he believes we can speed up our eternal process of development. *The Laws of the Sun* shows the way to realize true happiness—a happiness that continues from this world through the other.

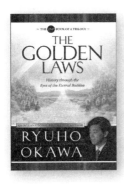

The Golden Laws

History through the Eyes of
the Eternal Buddha

E-book • 204 pages • $13.99
ISBN: 978-1-941779-82-8 (Sep. 24, 2015)

Throughout history, Great Guiding Spirits of Light have been present on Earth in both the East and the West at crucial points in human history to further our spiritual development. *The Golden Laws* reveals how the Divine Plan has been unfolding on Earth, and outlines 5,000 years of the secret history of humankind. Once we understand the true course of history, through past, present, and into the future, we cannot help but become aware of the significance of our spiritual mission in the present age.

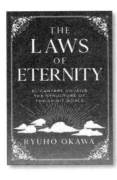

The Laws of Eternity

El Cantare Unveils the Structure of the
Spirit World

Paperback • 224 pages • $17.95
ISBN: 978-1-958655-16-0 (May 15, 2024)

"Where do we come from and where do we go after death?"
This unparalleled book offers us complete answers to life's most important questions that we all are confronted with at some point or another.
This book reveals the eternal mysteries and the ultimate secrets of Earth's Spirit Group that have been covered by the veil of legends and myths. Encountering the long-hidden Eternal Truths that are revealed for the first time in human history will change the way you live your life now.

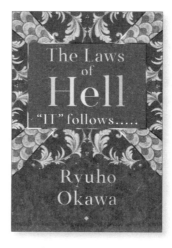

The Laws of Hell

"IT" follows.....

Paperback • 264 pages • $17.95
ISBN: 978-1-958655-04-7 (May 1, 2023)

Whether you believe it or not, the Spirit World and hell do exist. Currently, the Earth's population has exceeded 8 billion, and unfortunately, 1 in 2 people are falling to hell.

This book is a must-read at a time like this since more and more people are unknowingly heading to hell; the truth is, new areas of hell are being created, such as 'internet hell' and 'hell on earth.' Also, due to the widespread materialism, there is a sharp rise in the earthbound spirits wandering around Earth because they have no clue about the Spirit World.

To stop hell from spreading and to save the souls of all human beings, Ryuho Okawa has compiled vital teachings in this book. This publication marks his 3,100th book and is the one and only comprehensive Truth about the modern hell.

Recommended Books

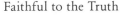

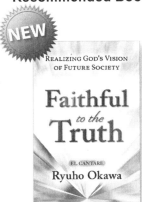

Faithful to the Truth
Realizing God's Vision of Future Society

Paperback • 164 pages • $20.00
ISBN: 979-8-887371-12-2 (Apr. 24, 2024)

The spiritual truth and the forecasts written in this book are messages from God that people worldwide should know right now. The world is on the verge of collapse. So, now is the time when people should listen to what Okawa is saying, as he is the one who knows the Truth, who can see God's vision, and who is trying to guide humanity in the right direction.

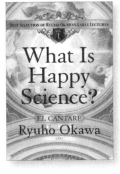

What Is Happy Science?
Best Selection of Ryuho Okawa's Early Lectures (Volume 1)

Paperback • 256 pages • $17.95
ISBN: 978-1-942125-99-0 (Aug. 25, 2023)

The Best Selection series is a collection of Ryuho Okawa's passionate lectures from the ages of 32 to 33 that reveal the mission and goal of Happy Science. This book contains the eternal Truth, including the meaning of life, the secret of the mind, the true meaning of love, the mystery of the universe, and how to end hatred and world conflicts.

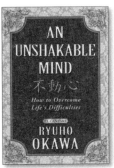

An Unshakable Mind
How to Overcome Life's Difficulties

Paperback • 180 pages • $17.95
ISBN:978-1-942125-91-4 (Nov. 30, 2023)

This book will guide you to build the genuine self-confidence necessary to shape a resilient character and withstand life's turbulence. Ryuho Okawa breaks down the causes of life's difficulties and provides solutions to overcome them from the spiritual viewpoint of life based on the laws of the mind.

Words of Wisdom Series

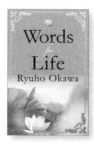

Words for Life

Paperback • 136 pages • $15.95
ISBN: 979-8-88727-089-7 (Mar. 16, 2023)

Ryuho Okawa has written over 3,150 books on various topics. To help readers find the teachings that are beneficial for them out of the extensive teachings, the author has written 100 phrases and put them together. Inside you will find words of wisdom that will help you improve your mindset and lead you to live a meaningful and happy life.

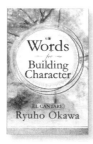

Words for Building Character

Paperback • 140 pages • $15.95
ISBN: 979-8-88737-091-0 (Jun. 21, 2023)

When your life comes to an end, what you can bring with you to the other world is your enlightenment, in other words, the character that you build in this lifetime. If you can read, relish, and truly understand the meaning of these religious phrases, you will be able to attain happiness that transcends this world and the next.

Words to Read in Times of Illness

Hardcover • 136 pages • $17.95
ISBN: 978-1-958655-07-8 (Sep. 15, 2023)

Ryuho Okawa has written 100 Healing Messages to comfort the souls of those going through any illness. When we are ill, it is an ideal time for us to contemplate recent and past events, as well as our relationship with the people around us. It is a chance for us to take inventory of our emotions and thoughts.

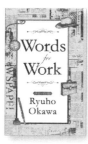

Words for Work

Paperback • 140 pages • $15.95
ISBN: 979-8-88737-090-3 (Jul. 20, 2023)

Through his personal experiences at work, Okawa has created these phrases regarding philosophies and practical wisdom about work. This book will be of great use to you throughout your career. Every day you can contemplate and gain tips on how to better your work as well as deepen your insight into company management.

MUSIC BY RYUHO OKAWA

A song celebrating Lord God / With Savior

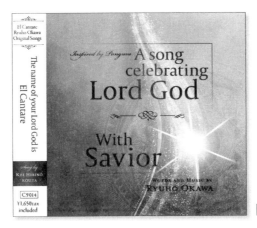

Words & Music by Ryuho Okawa

1. A song celebrating Lord God—Renewal ver.
2. With Savior —Renewal ver.
3. A song celebrating Lord God— Renewal ver. (Instrumental)
4. With Savior —Renewal ver. (Instrumental)
5. With Savior —Renewal ver. (Instrumental with chorus)

WHO IS EL CANTARE?

El Cantare means "the Light of the Earth." He is the Supreme God of the Earth who has been guiding humankind since the beginning of Genesis, and He is the Creator of the universe. He is whom Jesus called Father and Muhammad called Allah, and is *Ame-no-Mioya-Gami*, Japanese Father God. Different parts of
El Cantare's core consciousness have descended to Earth in the past, once as Alpha and another as Elohim. His branch spirits, such as Shakyamuni Buddha and Hermes, have descended to Earth many times and helped to flourish many civilizations. To unite various religions and to integrate various fields of study in order to build a new civilization on Earth, a part of the core consciousness has descended to Earth as Master Ryuho Okawa.

Alpha is a part of the core consciousness of El Cantare who descended to Earth around 330 million years ago. Alpha preached Earth's Truths to harmonize and unify Earth-born humans and space people who came from other planets.

Elohim is a part of the core consciousness of El Cantare who descended to Earth around 150 million years ago. He gave wisdom, mainly on the differences between light and darkness, good and evil.

Ame-no-Mioya-Gami (Japanese Father God) is the Creator God and the Father God who appears in ancient literature, *Hotsuma Tsutae*. It is believed that He descended on the foothills of Mt. Fuji about 30,000 years ago and built the Fuji dynasty, which is the root of the Japanese civilization. With justice as the central pillar, Ame-no-Mioya-Gami's teachings spread to ancient civilizations of other countries in the world.

Shakyamuni Buddha was born as a prince into the Shakya clan in India around 2,600 years ago. When he was 29 years old, he renounced the world and sought enlightenment. He later attained Great Enlightenment and founded Buddhism.

Hermes is one of the 12 Olympian gods in Greek mythology, but the spiritual Truth is that he taught the teachings of love and progress around 4,300 years ago which became the origin of the current Western civilization. He is a hero who truly existed.

Ophealis was born in Greece around 6,500 years ago and was the leader who took an expedition as far as Egypt. He is the God of miracles, prosperity, and arts, and is known as Osiris in Egyptian mythology.

Rient Arl Croud was born as a king of the ancient Incan Empire around 7,000 years ago and taught about the mysteries of the mind. In the heavenly world, he is responsible for the interactions that take place between various planets.

Thoth was an almighty leader who built the golden age of the Atlantic civilization around 12,000 years ago. In Egyptian mythology, he is known as God Thoth.

Ra Mu was a leader who built the golden age of the civilization of Mu around 17,000 years ago. As a religious leader and a politician, he ruled by uniting religion and politics.

ABOUT HAPPY SCIENCE

Happy Science is a religious group founded on the faith in El Cantare who is the God of the Earth, and the Creator of the universe. The essence of human beings is the soul that was created by God, and we all are children of God. God is our true parent, so in our souls, we have a fundamental desire to "believe in God, love God, and get closer to God." And, we can get closer to God by living with God's Will as our own. In Happy Science, we call this the "Exploration of Right Mind." More specifically, it means to practice the Fourfold Path, which consists of "Love, Wisdom, Self-Reflection, and Progress."

Love: Love means "love that gives," or mercy. God hopes for the happiness of all people. Therefore, living with God's Will as our own means to start by practicing "love that gives."

Wisdom: By studying and putting spiritual knowledge into practice, you can cultivate wisdom and become better at resolving problems in life.

Self-Reflection: Once you learn the heart of God and the difference between His mind and yours, you should strive to bring your own mind closer to the mind of God—that process is called self-reflection. Self-reflection also includes meditation and prayer.

Progress: Since God hopes for the happiness of all people, you should also make progress in your love, and make an effort to realize utopia in which everyone in your society, country, and eventually all humankind can become happy.

As we practice this Fourfold Path, our souls will advance toward God step by step. That is when we can attain real happiness— our souls' desire to get closer to God comes true.

In Happy Science, we conduct activities to make ourselves happy through belief in Lord El Cantare, and to spread this faith to the world and bring happiness to all. We welcome you to join our activities!

We hold events and activities to help you practice the Fourfold Path at our branches, temples, missionary centers and missionary houses

Love: We hold various volunteering activities. Our members conduct missionary work together as the greatest practice of love.

Wisdom: We offer our comprehensive collection of books of Truth, many of which are available online and at Happy Science locations. In addition, we offer numerous opportunities such as seminars or book clubs to learn the Truth.

Self-Reflection: We offer opportunities to polish your mind through self-reflection, meditation, and prayer. Many members have experienced improvement in their human relationships by changing their own minds.

Progress: We also offer seminars to enhance your power of influence. Because it is also important to do well at work to make society better, we hold seminars to improve your work and management skills.

"The True Words Spoken By Buddha"

"The True Words Spoken By Buddha" is an English sutra given directly from the spirit of Shakyamuni Buddha, who is a part of Master Ryuho Okawa's subconscious. The words in this sutra are not of a mere human being but are the words of God or Buddha sent directly from the ninth dimension, which is the highest realm of the Earth's Spirit World.

"The True Words Spoken By Buddha" is an essential sutra for us to connect and live with God or Buddha's Will as our own.

MEMBERSHIPS

MEMBERSHIP

If you would like to know more about Happy Science, please consider becoming a member. Those who pledge to believe in Lord El Cantare and wish to learn more can join us.

When you become a member, you will receive the following sutras: "The True Words Spoken By Buddha," "Prayer to the Lord" and "Prayer to Guardian and Guiding Spirits."

DEVOTEE MEMBER

If you would like to learn the teachings of Happy Science and walk the path of faith, become a Devotee member who pledges devotion to the Three Treasures, which are Buddha, Dharma, and Sangha. Buddha refers to Lord El Cantare, Master Ryuho Okawa. Dharma refers to Master Ryuho Okawa's teachings. Sangha refers to Happy Science. Devoting to the Three Treasures will let your Buddha nature shine, and you will enter the path to attain true freedom of the mind.

Becoming a devotee means you become Buddha's disciple. You will discipline your mind and act to bring happiness to society.

✉ EMAIL OR ☎ PHONE CALL
Please turn to the contact information page.

🔊 ONLINE member.happy-science.org/signup/ 🔍

CONTACT INFORMATION

Happy Science is a worldwide organization with branches and temples around the globe. For full details, visit happy-science.org. The following are some of our main Happy Science locations:

UNITED STATES AND CANADA

New York
79 Franklin St., New York, NY 10013, USA
Phone: 1-212-343-7972
Fax: 1-212-343-7973
Email: ny@happy-science.org
Website: happyscience-usa.org

New Jersey
66 Hudson St., #2R, Hoboken, NJ 07030, USA
Phone: 1-201-313-0127
Email: nj@happy-science.org
Website: happyscience-usa.org

Chicago
2300 Barrington Rd., Suite #400,
Hoffman Estates, IL 60169, USA
Phone: 1-630-937-3077
Email: chicago@happy-science.org
Website: happyscience-usa.org

Florida
5208 8th St., Zephyrhills, FL 33542, USA
Phone: 1-813-715-0000
Fax: 1-813-715-0010
Email: florida@happy-science.org
Website: happyscience-usa.org

Atlanta
1874 Piedmont Ave., NE Suite 360-C
Atlanta, GA 30324, USA
Phone: 1-404-892-7770
Email: atlanta@happy-science.org
Website: happyscience-usa.org

San Francisco
525 Clinton St.
Redwood City, CA 94062, USA
Phone & Fax: 1-650-363-2777
Email: sf@happy-science.org
Website: happyscience-usa.org

Los Angeles
1590 E. Del Mar Blvd., Pasadena,
CA 91106, USA
Phone: 1-626-395-7775
Fax: 1-626-395-7776
Email: la@happy-science.org
Website: happyscience-usa.org

Orange County
16541 Gothard St. Suite 104
Huntington Beach, CA 92647
Phone: 1-714-659-1501
Email: oc@happy-science.org
Website: happyscience-usa.org

San Diego
7841 Balboa Ave. Suite #202
San Diego, CA 92111, USA
Phone: 1-626-395-7775
Fax: 1-626-395-7776
E-mail: sandiego@happy-science.org
Website: happyscience-usa.org

Hawaii
Phone: 1-808-591-9772
Fax: 1-808-591-9776
Email: hi@happy-science.org
Website: happyscience-usa.org

Kauai
3343 Kanakolu Street, Suite 5
Lihue, HI 96766, USA
Phone: 1-808-822-7007
Fax: 1-808-822-6007
Email: kauai-hi@happy-science.org
Website: happyscience-usa.org

Toronto

845 The Queensway
Etobicoke, ON M8Z 1N6, Canada
Phone: 1-416-901-3747
Email: toronto@happy-science.org
Website: happy-science.ca

Vancouver

#201-2607 East 49th Avenue,
Vancouver, BC, V5S 1J9, Canada
Phone: 1-604-437-7735
Fax: 1-604-437-7764
Email: vancouver@happy-science.org
Website: happy-science.ca

INTERNATIONAL

Tokyo

1-6-7 Togoshi, Shinagawa,
Tokyo, 142-0041, Japan
Phone: 81-3-6384-5770
Fax: 81-3-6384-5776
Email: tokyo@happy-science.org
Website: happy-science.org

London

3 Margaret St.
London, W1W 8RE United Kingdom
Phone: 44-20-7323-9255
Fax: 44-20-7323-9344
Email: eu@happy-science.org
Website: www.happyscience-uk.org

Sydney

516 Pacific Highway, Lane Cove North,
2066 NSW, Australia
Phone: 61-2-9411-2877
Fax: 61-2-9411-2822
Email: sydney@happy-science.org

Sao Paulo

Rua. Domingos de Morais 1154,
Vila Mariana, Sao Paulo SP
CEP 04010-100, Brazil
Phone: 55-11-5088-3800
Email: sp@happy-science.org
Website: happyscience.com.br

Jundiai

Rua Congo, 447, Jd. Bonfiglioli
Jundiai-CEP, 13207-340, Brazil
Phone: 55-11-4587-5952
Email: jundiai@happy-science.org

Seoul

74, Sadang-ro 27-gil,
Dongjak-gu, Seoul, Korea
Phone: 82-2-3478-8777
Fax: 82-2-3478-9777
Email: korea@happy-science.org

Taipei

No. 89, Lane 155, Dunhua N. Road,
Songshan District, Taipei City 105, Taiwan
Phone: 886-2-2719-9377
Fax: 886-2-2719-5570
Email: taiwan@happy-science.org

Taichung

No. 146, Minzu Rd., Central Dist.,
Taichung City 400001, Taiwan
Phone: 886-4-22233777
Email: taichung@happy-science.org

Kuala Lumpur

No 22A, Block 2, Jalil Link Jalan Jalil Jaya
2, Bukit Jalil 57000,
Kuala Lumpur, Malaysia
Phone: 60-3-8998-7877
Fax: 60-3-8998-7977
Email: malaysia@happy-science.org
Website: happyscience.org.my

Kathmandu

Kathmandu Metropolitan City,
Ward No. 15, Ring Road, Kimdol,
Sitapaila Kathmandu, Nepal
Phone: 977-1-537-2931
Email: nepal@happy-science.org

Kampala

Plot 877 Rubaga Road, Kampala
P.O. Box 34130 Kampala, UGANDA
Email: uganda@happy-science.org

ABOUT IRH PRESS USA INC.

Founded in 2013, New York-based IRH Press USA, Inc. is the North American affiliate of IRH Press Co., Ltd., Japan. The Press exclusively publishes comprehensive titles on Spiritual Truth, religious enrichment, Buddhism, personal growth, and contemporary commentary by Ryuho Okawa, the author of more than 3,150 unique publications, with hundreds of millions of copies sold worldwide. For more information, visit Okawabooks.com.

Follow us on:

f Facebook: Okawa Books   **◎** Instagram: OkawaBooks

▶ Youtube: Okawa Books   **🐦** Twitter: Okawa Books

𝓟 Pinterest: Okawa Books   **g** Goodreads: Ryuho Okawa

——— **NEWSLETTER** ———

To receive book-related news, promotions and events, please subscribe to our newsletter below.

∞ irhpress.com/pages/subscribe

——— **AUDIO / VISUAL MEDIA** ———

YOUTUBE

PODCAST

Learn more of Happy Science teachings; topics ranging from self-help, current affairs, spirituality, religion, and the universe.